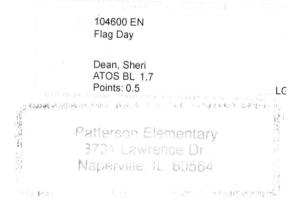

104600 EN
Flag Day

Dean, Sheri
ATOS BL 1.7
Points: 0.5

LG

WEEKLY **WR** READER
EARLY LEARNING LIBRARY

Our Country's Holidays

Flag Day

by Sheri Dean

Reading consultant: Susan Nations, M.Ed.,
author/literacy coach/
consultant in literacy development

Please visit our web site at: www.earlyliteracy.cc
For a free color catalog describing Weekly Reader® Early Learning Library's list
of high-quality books, call 1-877-445-5824 (USA) or 1-800-387-3178 (Canada).
Weekly Reader® Early Learning Library's fax: (414) 336-0164.

Library of Congress Cataloging-In-Publication Data

Dean, Sheri.
    Flag day / by Sheri Dean.
       p. cm. — (Our country's holidays)
    Includes bibliographical references and index.
    ISBN 0-8368-6504-9 (lib. bdg.)
    ISBN 0-8368-6511-1 (softcover)
    1. Flag Day—Juvenile literature. I. Title.
  JK1761.D43   2006
  394.263—dc22   2005032010

This edition first published in 2006 by
Weekly Reader® Early Learning Library
A Member of the WRC Media Family of Companies
330 West Olive Street, Suite 100
Milwaukee, WI 53212 USA

Copyright © 2006 by Weekly Reader® Early Learning Library

Managing editor: Valerie J. Weber
Art direction: Tammy West
Cover design and page layout: Kami Strunsee
Picture research: Cisley Celmer

Picture credits: Cover, © White Cross Productions/Getty Images; p. 5 © Gary Randall/Getty Images;
p. 7 © Gary Conner/PhotoEdit; p. 9 © Joel Sartore/National Geographic Image Collection; p. 11
© Stephen Simpson/Getty Images; p. 13 © Tom Carter/PhotoEdit; p. 15 © Tony Freeman/PhotoEdit;
p. 17 © Skjold Photographs; p. 19 © Gibson Stock Photography; p. 21 © Lilly Dong/Getty Images

Printed in the United States of America

1 2 3 4 5 6 7 8 9 10 09 08 07 06

Note to Educators and Parents

Reading is such an exciting adventure for young children! They are beginning to integrate their oral language skills with written language. To encourage children along the path to early literacy, books must be colorful, engaging, and interesting; they should invite the young reader to explore both the print and the pictures.

In *Our Country's Holidays*, children learn how the holidays they celebrate in their families and communities are observed across our nation. Using lively photographs and simple prose, each title explores a different national holiday and explains why it is significant.

Each book is specially designed to support the young reader in the reading process. The familiar topics are appealing to young children and invite them to read — and reread — again and again. The full-color photographs and enhanced text further support the student during the reading process.

In addition to serving as wonderful picture books in schools, libraries, homes, and other places where children learn to love reading, these books are specifically intended to be read within an instructional guided reading group. This small group setting allows beginning readers to work with a fluent adult model as they make meaning from the text. After children develop fluency with the text and content, the book can be read independently. Children and adults alike will find these books supportive, engaging, and fun!

— Susan Nations, M.Ed., author, literacy coach,
and consultant in literacy development

Flag Day is the birthday
of our flag!

Every country has a flag.

Our flag stands for the

United States of America.

Red, white, and blue are the special colors of our flag. Fifty stars and thirteen stripes are on our flag.

Flag Day is always on June 14. Many people fly an American flag on this day.

On Flag Day, Americans honor their flag and their country. Some people watch parades.

There are special rules about caring for the flag. We fold our worn flags and put them away. New flags go up.

The flag should never touch the ground.

Our flag should always fly higher than any other flag around it.

19

On Flag Day, we put out our flag. We are proud to be Americans!

Glossary

American — a person from the United States of America

country — the land that forms a nation

honor — to show respect

proud — to be very pleased about something

For More Information

Books

F Is For Flag. Reading Railroad Books (series). Wendy Cheyette Lewiston (Grosset & Dunlap)

Flag Day. National Holidays (series). Mari C. Schuh (Pebble Books)

Flag Day. Rookie Read-About Holidays (series). Kelly Bennett. (Children's Press)

What Freedom Means to Me: A Flag Day Story. Heather French Henry (Cubbie Blue Publishing)

Web Sites

Betsy Ross Home Page
www.ushistory.org/betsy/flagpics.html
Read about the different flags the United States has used throughout its history.

Index

About the Author

Sheri Dean is a school librarian in Milwaukee, Wisconsin. She was an elementary school teacher for fourteen years. She enjoys introducing books and information to curious children and adults.